Burning Bright

Book One of the Life Collection Series

Suzanne Stone

authorHOUSE®

AuthorHouse™ UK Ltd.
500 Avebury Boulevard
Central Milton Keynes, MK9 2BE
www.authorhouse.co.uk
Phone: 08001974150

First published by AuthorHouse 6/2/2009

ISBN: 978-1-4389-5622-0 (sc)

Printed in the United States of America
Bloomington, Indiana

This book is printed on acid-free paper.

Artwork by Paris Cannon
Photography by Troy Cannon

This book is dedicated to my husband, my ongoing project
and inspiration.....
To my three sons, who have provided me with subjects
and the ability to be ever patient.....
To my parents who have helped me become
the woman that I am.....

to all with love.

Contents

Foreword

In my life's travels the road has taken me many places. As a result I have had the opportunity to meet many different people from all walks of life. Sometimes it is just a friendly nod or a brief hello on many occasions lasting friendships were formed.

During Police Week in 2002, I met P.C. Winn from Staffordshire, England at the National Law Enforcement Officers Memorial in Washington D.C. This chance meeting, which started out with words of thanks and mutual respect, forged an honored and lasting friendship.

I sensed immediately his devotion to our Police profession and his pride of serving others. It was amazing to me to learn how much we had in common and how we shared the same values and concerns.

Months later he brought his wife across the pond to experience the comradeship and love that is shared during Police Week. It is an emotional roller coaster as we greet old friends and pay tribute to fellow Officers that made the Ultimate Sacrifice in the Line of Duty.

Upon meeting P.C. Winn's wife (Author Suzanne Stone) I felt as though we were old friends and conversation came easy. It was obvious to me that she was Winn's foundation and source of strength. She seemed to have a great understanding of her spiritual self. She also displayed wit and spunky humor with a very British accent that brought smiles to our faces during a very somber week.

Over the past few years my wife and I have come to know Suzanne Stone even more. She and her husband are dear friends. We have shared our family's joys, triumphs, and sorrows. We were pleased to have

5

Suzanne and her husband spend holiday at our home in Michigan.

Suzanne Stone is a woman of great strength with a love for her family and her heritage. She exudes an inner peace that is felt by those around her. She has the ability to listen to her inner voice and see things from a different perspective and is able to translate her experiences into words.

As a people in today's world we have all experienced life's joys, sorrows, and disappointment. Suzanne Stone has put all these emotions in perspective in this collection of poems. As I read through each one I found myself thinking, Hey, I've been there; I felt that; wow! she understands. I laughed, I cried, I felt comfort. I believe you will too.

Captain Douglas R. Mills (retired)
Criminal Investigations Division Commander
Special Investigations Division Commander
Honor Guard Commander
Charter Township of Clinton Police Department
Clinton Township, Michigan.

Introduction

About the Author,

Suzanne Stones' parents migrated out of the inner city of Birmingham, England during the early 1960's. As children they had witnessed the Second World War and the hardships entwined within such an era.

They took the bold step to move out of city life and settled a few miles north, in the Cathedral city of Lichfield in Staffordshire, where they set up home and started family life.

In time they had three children of their own, Stone being the eldest, with a younger brother and sister. Stone attended the local primary school and then completed her education at the nearby Secondary High School.

She describes her childhood as a wonderful time, spent within a safe environment, much to the credit of her parent's efforts.

At the age of 17, Stone commenced work at the local library and later moved into the media. She spent 14 years working for a local independent newspaper, moving from reception, telesales, features coordination and eventually into field sales.

In 1985, she married her fiancé, who lived only two streets away as a boy, and whom had attended the same schools.

These two soul mates, in time, became parents to three boys.

Enjoying motherhood, Stone found time to hold down full time employment and time to diarise her experiences, on occasion using such material to have single poems published.

During the Nineties, Stone entered a new phase in her life, finding employment in the world of horticulture, working within a small wholesale garden nursery. In part, this was due to a love of the outdoors, encouraged in no doubt, by her parent's life long passion to garden.

The work was tough, yet still enjoyable, working outside in the fields during all weathers. In time the successful nursery expanded into the retail sector.

Having earned her stripes over the seasons out in the fields, Stone was offered the chance to move into the calmer atmosphere of the retail garden centre. An opportunity she decided, not to be missed. In dealing directly with members of the public, she was now able to accelerate her knowledge of all things plants.

She had found another topic to write about, the seasons, and her favourite flowers, they all became characters within her diaries and poems.

In 2007, after more than eight years, came the time for a change of direction. Realising that progress within the small family business was not going to be an option, Stone reluctantly made the decision to move on. With her sons becoming more independent there was now opportunity to utilise the free time on her hands.

Stone spent a year taking up different part-time jobs and set about reorganising her life. Evaluating her notebooks and diarised experiences during previous and current times had provided a rich source of material for the future. From such archives came a piece of observational work entitled "Shopping Days". Penned in September 2008, it has just made it into this book in time, a hint of things to come.

One could describe Stone as a home-girl with her roots firmly fixed in Lichfield, yet, she has continued to travel when opportunities arise. During the last decade, Stone has regularly travelled across the Atlantic to North America and Canada, along with regular trips south to the Spanish Canary Islands. Such travel has provided for a significant amount of experiences to be recorded in her multitude of notebooks and in turn found their way into verse.

Stone's husband is a UK Police Officer, and as vacations permit they travel to Washington D.C. to attend and participate in the annual Police Week ceremonies and memorials. (www.nleomf.com).

During such experiences, Stone has been fortunate to make friendships with Americans. They have welcomed and invited her family into their lives and homes across the continent.

Such encounters have enabled Stone precious time with US Police families and given her the encouragement to write about differing perceptions of loss and the pain endured within such relationships.

In May of 2007, the poem Burning Bright was orated for the first time to a small audience consisting of Police honor/honour guard families from the Charter Township of Clinton Police at the home of Nancy and Peter Mackenzie, in Shelby Township, Michigan. Genuine people who knew only too well of the experiences of loss of a loved one, friend or colleague.

The positive reaction to that poem caused Stone to reveal the extent of her extraordinary private repertoire and to gain the confidence to produce this, her debut book. Herein, is an anthology of poems from across different spectres of her life, coupled with individual forewords and some photographic and hand drawn images of perspective.

As this book heads to print, Stone is already busy on her sequel entitled "My Place".

Burning Bright

Each life should burn as bright as it can whilst it can; we all have the ability to shine, maybe if only for a while. We, each and every one of us are capable of glowing in some way. We just need to allow ourselves the freedom to ignite the flame inside.

When we are low our flame just flickers, only to be lit up when we are feeling bright and carefree. I truly believe we can all burn bright somehow.

There are also many flames lit upon this earth which are so short lived, or have their spark extinguished far too soon. It is my belief that we can keep the light they have left behind alight. This light can be carried within our hearts, gently glowing, until we meet again.

Therefore, I leave you with this thought, never willingly let your own flame go out, even if it only flickers silently for years, there will be a moment in time or a second in your life when you must allow it to burn bright,

Happy thoughts,

Suzanne Stone

Emotions

Burning Bright

A time to reflect, ...in the lighting of this candle, and the burning of the flame. Let us remember those that have gone before us, and let us think of those who continue to serve and protect us.

Since 2002, I have been fortunate to attend a number of emotional gatherings and memorial services both in the UK and the USA in respect of fallen Police officers.

During one occasion in my hometown of Lichfield, in England, I met with families from Northern Ireland. We each held lighted candles whilst my husband recited some words. I was privileged to experience moments of reflection of the most private and intimate kind at that time.

I witnessed how these families gained strength from such moments.

This poem was inspired by such experience. On being touched to the core it has left an everlasting impression upon my soul.

My thoughts go out to all families, friends and colleagues of the honoured men and women of the armed forces, police and emergency services whom give the ultimate sacrifice.

Burning Bright

See this candle burning bright
See its flame of dancing light
Feel its warmth and see its glow
Let it's light through, the darkness show

Lighting up the saddened heart
Moving away clouds, keeping you apart
Of those you've loved and lost before
With ease, be silent, and remember once more

To a time of joy and happiness
A place of peace and calm
Knowing now in silence
They are free from harm

In life they touched you deeply
In death that will remain
You had their love completely
This will always be the same

Let them go without regret
The life they had was good
In time we know we will not forget
We are sure we never would

Take this candle burning bright
See its flame of dancing light
Feel its warmth and see its glow
Hold it there for today, and your tomorrows.

ghosts

Strong feelings, and mixed up emotions within this poem.
I have this belief, just maybe, not all ghosts are the same.

Here I have strived to detail a way through to clear thoughts and brighter days.

Ghosts

A moment, a place, a stillness of time
A precious amendment to life's burly brine
Remember the ghost that was once you
The person you left far behind
Sit back and greet him contentedly
Let him take over not hide
For he is our self, we need to let free
In times of trouble and disharmony
With the world or our lovers
Ourselves or our friends
Let this ghost in, for he'll make amends

Behind the rain, follows the sun
Behind ourselves emerges the one
We must let out a graceful cry
Do not let this time die
Keep hold, grip on tight
Do not let go without a fight
For our ghost is the courier of times to unfold
Become again rich in feelings of old

Beware of the ghost holding the devil within
He's only there to cast doubt with a grin
He is the one with deep dark eyes
This ghost won't allow you through to blue skies
These are our memories of bad times and sorrow
Don't stay in this place, seek out tomorrow
Hiding in corners is his favourite thing
Waiting to pounce, not to let your heart sing

Let loose and reach, beyond the darkened day
Shout them out and into the haze
Times of joy must now prevail
Troubled moments we must avail
The ghost he is our brightening star
A glow from the past, a light from afar
Seize him now and hold on tight
He'll guide you through your darkest night.

Land of the Indian Chief

There are times when I only need to hear a piece of music, such as Native American music and song, in order to trigger my verse.

The relaxing, methodical tempo takes me to a place where I can picture the environment and feel the atmosphere.

Land of the Indian Chief is an emotive poem, concerning the subject of mortality and how I envisage it maybe faced.

Land of the Indian Chief

See the great chief, what silent command
His face etched with life, he's part of this land

So silent his thoughts, his memories run deep
Once treading the soil, from meadow to creek

The silent emotions, reflect through blues eyes
His soul to reach out, and soar up to the skies

Wrapped in a cloak, to keep his bones warm
Hold onto this life, his decision now torn

His ancestors wait, so soon he must leave
Leaving his family, it's their time to grieve

Watching, as nature bore the open plains
He saw her avail, with cool breeze and fresh rain

So simple and strong, her emotions ran high
Mountainous ranges, where great eagles fly

The breath from his body, takes its last draw
He closes his eyes, and feels his heart soar

His soul flies free, a young brave once again
Running in fields and meadows he reigns.

Autumn Breeze

Vibrant autumn, in the presence of the falling sun....

I believe this poem should be read during an early autumn evening as the clear day turns to twilight.

Capture these words and let them wrap around you like a warm protective cloak.

Autumn Breeze

As the cool breeze whips around my feet
Moving up towards my hair
Autumn time I now must greet
With zest and charm and dare

I feel lonely now and insecure
Why? I do not know
Beneath my veil of calmness
The emotion begins to grow

Like the cool breeze it begins
Slowly, sensuously, creeping
A chill about my soul it stirs
Swirling, jumping, leaping

Around and around within me
Until it blows away
So now I'm left calm again
Until another day.

A Million Times

I find that experiences in my own life, that of my relatives, friends and world events, tug at my emotions and then I feel the urge to write.

During the months and years following September 11th 2001, the stories of the people caught up in the incidents of that fateful day in America began to emerge. With more information, came a deeper understanding for me, of the losses borne that day. Since those times and on experiencing sudden, shocking, unexpected, personal loss within my own family, I began to apprehend and negotiate these immense emotions for real.

I became motivated to write down words reflecting how I felt about my friend Madeline. When we first met I learned about the loss of her husband - Keith Neumann, an Essex County Police Officer in Irvington, New Jersey, USA.

After only six weeks of marriage Keith was tragically killed during a police operation.

I felt the cruelty of his death, when at such time in their lives; there had been so much optimism for the future.

The mixed emotions arising, gave me the drive to put together a piece of writing that originally, had been ticking away in my head.

I have endeavoured to capture deep feelings throughout the journey of loss, pain, and progressing recovery with this special, special poem.

A Million Times

A million times I wished I'd said
The things I did not say
A million times I'd wished I'd done
The things I did not do

Through all the years and all the days
Of all the times and all the ways
A million times I've cried since then
A million times I've died

I've been to a place within my soul
The coldest darkest deepest hole
A million times I'd wished I'd gone
A million times with you

The day you left is etched forever
Your face disappeared from view
A million times I've wondered why
A million questions asked with a sigh

Now time has calmed my anger
The days are filled with light
Emotions no longer reeling
And your face comes back to sight

With my fear and anger ebbing
I can begin to see
A million little hopes and dreams
A million ways to be

To live is to remember you
In every single way
Moving on is to honour you
With every passing day

A million times we laughed
A million times we cried
You are within my memory
So I can never hide

A million days I have to go
A million memories to be made
So many people yet to know
So through life now I must wade

Until the time we meet again
The time I'll hold you near
A million reasons to be brave
Facing all my challenges without fear

A million reasons I have to live
A million different days
With each and every one
I see clearly through the haze

A million times I remember
A million things we shared
So be silent now my darling
Your pain has now been spared.

Family

Call me Dad......

This poem is an interpretation of how I saw my husband during his emerging relationship with our first-born son.

I have attempted to capture a man moving into fatherhood.

Call me Dad......

When one can say "I'm a Dad"
Those words could never express
What I feel deep inside
Is more than joyful happiness
A son I have, what an honour
I carry this privilege about me
Like a proud and colourful banner
He's young just now, I must make it last
Watch him closely, teach him all I know
His youthful years will go so fast
I'll see he's strong, my pride will show

Now is the only time I can join him
And become again, a child
This opportunity I have been given
Can be joyful, forgetful and wild
Remembering how it used to be
When I was a youthful boy
Now my time has arrived, as will his
To become a father to my lad
To watch him move and grow
But still the proudest thing of all
Is to hear him call me "Dad".

Alexander

Albeit he is now an adult, standing taller than I, and likely not to forgive me, this poem is about our eldest son.

Alexander

He's charming, chatty, noisy and calm
Full of verve, whit and chance
We hope he never comes to harm
He's naughty, sleepy, rude and serene
He has dark hair and cherub lips
Full of talkative nonsensical quips
He's our Son that is true
Alexander is our baby, still brand new.

Gampa

When my Grandfather Alfred died I wrote this poem.
He had seen both World Wars and had travelled to some distant lands during his time in the military service.

I wrote this poem in an effort to interpret the relationship between my young son and his Great-Grandfather.

Gampa

Gampa was a special man
Although he never heard me say
I loved him only as a child can
In a very secret way

I'm not sad, now that he's gone
It doesn't mean the same to me
Because I'm a child, he'll always live on
In that special place, my memory

He saw my first steps, he heard me cry
He'd talk to me, I couldn't understand
I just knew that I should take his hand
Together we'd walk around his garden with pride
A small boy and his special guide

My Gampa's gone where it's quiet now
I know he loves me and he'll watch me grow
From a far away place we do not know
So Gampa if you're watching me
I know your face will light up with glee.

My Little Brother Dreams Away

Describing a time when one's children were young and everything was play, from when time seemed to fly by so quickly.

Written from the perspective of the older child, on the subject of the energetic younger brother!

My Little Brother Dreams Away

My little brothers' noisy, its true
But without him here, I don't know what I'd do
He's useful when I need to race
I love the way he laughs, a big smile upon his face

He's good at jumping on Moms' bed
Uh' oh, I hope he does not fall and bang his head
He's clever at getting sweets from Dad
"Not too many" Mom says, "It makes your teeth bad"

He can reach the biscuits upon high
If he could keep climbing, he'd reach the sky
Give him a big stick to 'whoosh' through the air
Better look out, he'll catch your legs right there

He can be quiet, playing with cars on the mat
He lines them all up, just like that
From Power Rangers, to Biker Mice from Mars
His day is a challenge, how to reach the stars

As Halloween approached, he was dressed all in red
Thank goodness, it's nearly time for the little devils' bed
It makes my heart rest at the end of a long hard day
To see my little brother sleep and watch him dream away.

I Recall

A recollection of a conversation I had with my Grandmother Violet, as I reached the ripe old age of 10!

I Recall

When I was ten
you asked me back then
"Do you feel any different now?"
"Yes I do," I thought, somehow

Lots of times we'd talk with Mom
then came the time when I became one
so glad you shared that joy with me
a Great-Grandson of yours, my new family

As I grew older I knew you more
a sad time came, when you knew us no more
I loved you then, I'll miss you now
reunited with Grandad on a peaceful bow.

My Brother

I wrote this piece and that of Where Tulips Grow (Seasons Chapter) for my husband.

In September 2008, my husband's younger brother, was tragically killed during a violent incident with, and by the hand of, his ex partner.

During the prevailing time of immense grief, I had this overwhelming emotional urge to write. Unearthed, from the memories, photographs, and stories that I knew my husband had shared with his younger brother.

With tears streaming, the love and the bonds are all too plain to see.

My Brother

We will think of you, in the dead of night
When it's cold outside, and you're out of sight

We will see your face, from a time before
We will greet you there, with an open door

We will laugh with you, when you're feeling low
From the days we shared, not so long ago

We will say your name, as we speak each day
Remembering you, in our own special way

We will send you love, and guiding words
To get you to a place, where it no longer hurts

We will always know how, it was meant to be
My Brother I love you, rest peacefully.

QUESTIONS

My Love

Thought provoking poems can conjure up huge emotions.

At times, there are things we need to talk about, and then at other times there are things we just need to take time to think about.

My Love

Where will I find you? Where will you be?
So long you have stood there, right next to me
How will you hear me when I call out your name?
I need you to know, it won't be the same

Whose hand shall I take, as I walk down the street?
I can't find your warmth, where can we meet?
Who shall I hold when I want to dance?
On a musical night, a time for romance

Where will you be to dry all my tears?
You won't be close, to ease all my fears
How can I seek you in the deep dark night?
Turn over to touch you, it just won't be right

Whose tea do I make, as I set out the cups?
Our chats over biscuits, I'll miss you so much
What will I laugh at? you're not there with me
Those carefree moments, no longer to be

You have been my world, my life, my dream
No longer to touch my cheek, it would seem
Be rested my love, in a quiet space
Make it your home and save me a place.

Life's Folly

Life is full of unanswered questions.
We do not always need to have answers.

Sometimes we only need the question and be to left to ponder....

Life's Folly

Life is but a single dimension
A journey of learning and ideas
A way through existence
Folly forsaking the years

No sooner has it begun
We have to learn to accept
That a journey through life
Is but a single and true concept

One way, one aim, one road
With many small journeys through
Is life's folly to foretell?
Dreams just may come true.

I Wonder

On driving my car down a familiar country lane recently, I was reminded of a road trip the family once made from Lichfield to Hertfordshire, England.

The memory was of being in the old family car. Travelling in daylight, along a straight, tree lined country lane.

I recall being in the back seat, daydreaming, asking myself all kinds of questions as I looked out at the passing trees.

I Wonder

I wonder at the trees, as we drive along the lanes
Standing there in silence, I wonder, from where they came?

I wonder at the stories, if only they could speak?
Still standing there in silence, I listen as they creak

I wonder how they stay alone in just one place?
Could it be they're happy no need to move apace?

I wonder do they cry as they turn towards the land?
Only to see it shrinking, giving way to bricks and sand

I wonder are they wise? They look as though they are
Years of observations, peering in, on all the cars

I wonder if at night they look up towards the skies?
Do they feel the need to up root and go and hide?

I wonder as we pass, if tomorrow they'll be there?
For, I shall come again, along this lane, to where?

Silence

Lichfield, the historical home of Dr Samuel Johnson, Erasmus Darwin, and Saint Chad to name but a few, beholds a great jewel sitting quietly in the medieval Close.

Lichfield Cathedral annually attracts pilgrims from all over the world; her Three Spires acting like beacons reaching up into the sky.

Throughout my life I have been drawn to this magnificent building and many times I have wondered at its features and treasures. Despite the mighty bells announcing Evensong as such, and the overtones of the great organ within, she often stands silent, leaving one without distraction, yet amazed at her beauty.

After listening to a particular haunting piece of music, I felt myself being placed within the walls of Lichfield Cathedral. This holy building has always been of great interest to me. From a historical point of view there has been a religious building on this site for hundreds of years.

The poem encompasses my thoughts on what stories could be told if those spires and sacred walls could only speak!

Silence

Stand beneath the steeple, that reaches to the sky
Breath in the very history of ancient times gone by
Peer along its balconies, gargoyles balance there
So many years of turmoil, they witnessed without a care

This place is old and timeless, with historic tales to tell
Under Cromwell's armies, it very nearly fell
It's laboured troubles and conflicts, down it's many years
Seeing sights of sadness, troubles, and fears

Take a walk inside, where hallowed ground is found
Raise your head above, and take a look around
How majestic are its walls, sweeping up on high
See its stain glass windows, if only you could fly

Stay to light a candle, and reflect a moment here
For what ever you believe in, find that peace is near
So now our Lichfield Cathedral, has revealed to you it's past
It's shown how it drew them, and where the crowds amassed

You've seen its walls and tapestries, of history gone by
"Return again to see us" it's ghostly monks do cry
Whatever your religion, or what you perceive to be
Come visit once again, you'll be welcome with harmony.

Meditation

Boulders on the Sea

It has become a habit these days that I carry a notebook.

I have experienced that sometimes the written word comes by accident.

Over the years, I have found that if I stop for just a moment, I can take in my surroundings, and words come together inside my head.

On such occasion, whilst on holiday, sitting bedside the ocean, I penned "Boulders on the Sea".

Boulders on the Sea

I took a seat on the huge boulders, feeling as though invited
In my mind I versed, the words came, later to be recited
It was easy to sit, perched right there looking out to sea
So easy, watching life on the rocks, probably there watching me

As I sat a while, mesmerized by the lapping ocean at my feet
This is an opportunity I thought, to create, such a treat
No other thoughts invaded my head, time began to stand still
So I did, begin to write, like sitting on nature's windowsill

The rocks themselves, bold as brass, placed there neatly by man
No doubt someone sat here once, working out such a plan
A strategy, I thought, to hold back the trials of the sea upon the shore
A wise move of its time, an idea giving rise to many more

Forming a long spike out toward the aqua sea, it's purpose serves well
I suppose these large rocks stop, the ocean's great swell
These boulders placed here carefully, so neatly from the land
Before the sea would have clipped the beach, eating at the sand

The ocean itself a master of disguise, mostly calm here by the shore
But, when she feels the need, she can muster up quite a squall
Let her take you out to sea, play sometime upon her waves
I think of the heroes and the coastguards, all the lives to save

Quite remarkable, sitting upon my rock, looking out to sea
Happy and relaxed I feel, so calm my mind is set free
Taking time here, to think about the waves slapping against the sides
Let your emotions fly away like a bird, see how they glide

I watch as the tide flips over the rock pools below
I wonder if life underneath is disturbed, does it even know?
Swirling around, depositing froth on the surface like a good beer
Maybe it's peering back at me, thinking, life is fine, just here

I pull away my thoughts, from this timeless place
I wonder, did I leave an image on the water, of my face?
I wobble back to the beach, where we humans prefer to stand
So now my feet have landed, my toes on firmer land

My back is turned now, from the ocean so blue
I feel rested and honoured, now I know its true
I will return again when I need to leave my thoughts behind
The great expanse of water is as open as my mind.

Indian Spirit

I have always felt a deep emotional connection with nature and in particular with the Native American Indian.

Having one as my spirit guide, I have discovered a connection to my inner most emotions and that of nature's great offerings.

Every single day, we should be in touch with our inner spirit.

Practising Yoga for many years has enabled me to get in touch with this part of my soul, through deep relaxation and meditation.

Indian Spirit is my description of my soul running free.

When I read this poem, I tap to a repetitive rhythm and chant the words.

Indian Spirit

Indian Spirit, inside me
Waiting now, to be set free
Feel him call, to the open land
Where he will lead me, by the hand

Show me now, where the eagles fly
Take me there, to the clear blue sky
Chasing still and silent dreams
Of ancestral paths and running streams

Feel free breeze, upon my face
Through the tall grass, in a meadow we race
It's warm and clear and free inside
No longer will cold thoughts hide

See wild horses, galloping there
Faster, faster, without a care
A secret place, which has stood still
I'll drink it in, and take my fill

Face, the regal mountain range
A rugged land that will not change
Hear the sound, of my beating soul
The call of the wild, step out from the cold

Calming now, in a woodland place
Feel the cool air, upon my face
Sitting silent, beneath our tree
Indian Spirit, has been set free.

La Gomera, My Island of Dreams

Written, whilst on holiday on the Canary Island of Tenerife.

From the beach and even our apartment window, we could see the distant outline of the isle of La Gomera.

My imagination took over as I began to daydream about this quiet mystical island.

La Gomera, My Island of Dreams

Shrouded in the early morning mist, and covered by clouds
Still I see you, untouched from here, sun pulls away your shrouds

Do you have rolling hillsides of green? Or do you lay bare like me
Still I see you, untouched from here, way over there across the sea

I see you standing silent, rising above the sea, keeps me thinking
Still I see you, untouched from here, I stare over to you not blinking

You come into view, but not too much, only the top of your mountain
Still I see you, untouched from here, no longer am I doubting

The boats they sail across to you, I really don't feel the need
Still I see you, untouched from here, my imagination full fills my greed

So there you are, by night and by day, observed from afar by me
Still I see you, untouched from here, it's the way it will always be

The mist comes down, you are covered by clouds, hidden again it seems
Still I see you, untouched from here, La Gomera, my island of dreams.

Moments

Practising yoga is how I reach deep relaxation, visualization and by using calm words. This is one of my poems that I use during yoga meditation.

Moments

I recognise this place
It recognises me
It knows my reflective face
It knows I will not flee

A haunting sense of dejavu
I have stood here before
Surrounded by silence, all stands still
The madness of life no more

Gone are the moments of time
All things are balanced here
No ties, no bonds, no reason, or rhyme
I know this feeling without fear

Step one way to stillness
Step the other to noise
I know where lies calmness
I stand still now with poise

Breath in the air, pure and free
Feel it's freshness fill you up
I have this moment all for me
Take it in, drink from the cup

My heartbeat is gentle, feel as it slows
Neither see nor hear a single thing
From my feet to my head nature flows
My soul rises up, feel it sing

We all need moments, day by day
Somewhere to let time stand still
To take a breath and fade away
Climb down from the running mill

I recognise this place
And it recognises me
It's a very secret place
Which, only I can see.

My Little Place of Paradise

Escape is essential, even from our self.

I find to be out there with nature, is cathartic.

It solves so much.

My Little Place of Paradise

There is a place of paradise
where I really need to be
a little door to heaven
only there for me

This little place of paradise
is not so far from here
it is my place of paradise
where I can shed a tear

No one can see me crying
amongst my flowered friends
unobserved and silent
a place to make amends

No one to disturb, or call
to this little room of mine
for I will look to be enjoying
and they will never see a sign

This little place of paradise
is cream with lots of pink
it's where I go to solace
a place to be and think

This little place of paradise
I suppose, I can let you know
is my Potting Shed, so wonderful
in my garden where flowers grow.

Coffee Break Ditties

Healthy Competition

To compete is healthy
to take a challenge is broad of mind
to want to aspire is relentless
to forgive is natural
to love is everything.

Nancy's Mud

Nancy was a little girl
Built with ringlets and a nose that did curl
Nancy never looked a mess
She would stroll around just like a princess
Until one day, when Simon Fudd
Shoved her into a puddle of mud.

Ha Ha

Clive had a dream
That he was a soldier
Marching along the edge of a stream
When along came a big skittle, and bowled him over.

Salt and Pepper

Salt and Pepper
make the good things taste better
when your lay them out for tea.

Jigsaw, Jigsaw

Jigsaw, Jigsaw upon my floor
How you got there isn't a mystery at all
I took you from your box
I placed you down one by one
Then a picture grew of a brown fox
When he had a tail, I knew you were done.

21

You already have the key to my heart
Now here's the key to the door.

Realization

Our children are the future
That's what I have become
I've learnt how I must tutor
For I am now a mom.

Our Robin

I see the robin land, on our fence again
He visits every day, even in the rain
Our robin carries food in his beak
He whistles his tune, that's the way he speaks.

Forever

Forever I will want you
Every day I'll care
For each tomorrow, I'll need you
Just knowing you'll be there
Always and eternally, I'll love you
Much love and happiness
For our Wedding Day tomorrow.

Hope

The sun is here, the rain passed by
Stretch out your arms and reach for the sky
Do not be afraid when shadows fall
Take a moment to be calm and still, once more
Keep looking up, hold your head high
Stretch out your arms and reach for the sky
Your hopes and dreams, don't bury them down
Leave a smile on your face, and never a frown.

Observations

Shopping Days

Whilst working in a town centre clothes boutique, I had fun observing and talking with folk during their trials and tribulations of shopping for clothes.

Shopping being the centre of joy and excitement for so many ladies, it would also appear that husbands and partners have a slightly different experience during such events.

Shopping Days

It's windy today, as I watch them go by
Shopping bags full, carried with a sigh

Scanning the windows, for sales and trends
Money in wallets they need to spend

I like to watch them debate and decide
"Which colour to go for" What's on their mind?

Holding onto their hats and skirt hems down
Purchases to buy, all around town

Should it be striped? Should it be plain?
Can they wear short? Oh' what's the aim?

Ladies squeezing into tight jeans
"Not your size dear", so it would seem

Pastels, greens, purples and blues
So many shades, so many hues

See the men's faces, lost and drawn
Why is she buying that? It'll never be worn

Concede with a sigh, as lunch draws near
Oh' to sit down and rest my rear

To match the dress, the shoes she needs
"Please have them dear, they're great," he pleads

With many bags and heels worn down
Its time to go, and leave the town

Time to wait for their weekly pay
Soon to return, for another day.

The Boss

Written due to experience, in a previous career spanning 14 years worth of reception, advertisement and field sales work for a city newspaper.

My happy memories are of a media sales manager struggling to both control and manage his more experienced staff.

There were days when he thought he had won, and other days, when pushed, he had to simply close the office door.

The Boss

All we wanted was a smiling face
Not choice words, or a saving grace

A grin from one ear to the other would have done
Not a medley of natter about nothing, now't done

A simple crack upon the lips
Not a rally of nonsensical quips

A little gesture showing those white molars
Not a bear like façade of grumbles and growlers

So come on Boss smile at the workers
We're not just a bunch of hopeless shirkers.

Tenerife

Here, I set out my observations and experiences, as a tourist, of the activities and sights on the busy Canary Island, of Tenerife.

Tenerife

The lazy sun lifts quietly over the bare mountain regions
Exposing their imposing emptiness
Yellow flashes march across the skies like army legions

Releasing the hazy stillness of the early dawn
The skies free of the fluffy white clouds
A radiant azure blue over the early morn

The silence beneath breaks to murmurs and talk
Town folk below waft around their wares
As the tourists of Tenerife take their walks

The warmth from the sun starts to simmer and heat
Over the stalls and shopping parades
A bustle of early day purchases as visitors take to their feet

They descend to the sands on the beach
Overlooking the outstretched sea
With their towels and oil in hand they hurry to find a seat

Secluded under parasols to chatter and natter away
Languages no longer a barrier
Each person to relish their stay

Onto the sands come the ladies with their offers and wares
Some try to pretend they're asleep
Whilst others purchase the bananas and pears

The Chinese lady offers massage instead of buckets and spades
The Spanish gent some fruit or drink
Others your long hair they will braid

Aromas of food from the barbecues, float across the beach
Smell the homemade paella
A bustle of hungry patrons, ready to take their seat

As the day moves into siesta, it's time to take a rest
From the seething hot sun above
To retreat from the heat is the best

Boats on the ocean move away from the shore
Visitors taking a ride on the waves
The world beneath the surface has its magical draw

A sense of renewed activity, crawls across the town
From sleeping, sunbathing or shopping
All awakes to fresh sights and sounds

Nightlife beckons the young and old, come see
Freshly dressed and scented up
Walk, browse, shop, eat or simply just be

Tunes and music skate across the air to your ears
Laughter and fun all around
Simply no time for trouble or fears

Cast your eyes towards the sea
Ripples on the water sparkle
Feel rested, its such harmony

Walk along the waters edge breath in the ocean air
Lights in the distance shimmer
Your time, is now, you don't have a care

Tenerife closes now, for another day
The streets will slowly empty
We hope you enjoyed your stay.

PC WINN

A poem I wrote after invitation, and visit, to a wonderful kindergarten school in Richmond, Michigan whilst on holiday, in the USA.

My friend, and teacher at the school - Paulette Mills, arranged for my husband to meet the children after they had heard he was a Policeman back in England. Paulette's husband Doug is a retired Police Captain from nearby Charter Township of Clinton Police and together they thought the children would benefit from meeting a real life British "bobbie".

Aged around six years old, the children were full of questions for my husband who managed quite well with his geography and expression.

To the delight of the captivated children it must have appeared very odd to hear a quaint English accent, nonetheless, it held their attention.

This poem, a bit of fun, reminds me of all the chaotic activities being curtailed by a teacher as she brings the children into focus when a visitor comes a calling.............and goes out to all those Police School Liaison officers throughout the world making endeavours to get their message across to the next generation.

PC WINN

Pretty as a picture, Sally wipes her nose
Pretty as a picture, she steps on Joeys' toes
The wails and screams, are heard throughout the class
Miss Jolly spins around, to see the squabbling mass

She calms the situation, and cools down all the noise
"Stop chattering now girls" and rearranging all the boys
Sitting on the floor, they peer through beady eyes
Curiosity descends "Who could that be?" someone cries

Miss Jolly introduces, the attraction of the show
A big tall gentleman, with bright buttons all a glow
Removing his big tall hat, and showing a friendly grin
"Good morning children, my name is Pc Winn"

"Good morning Pc Winn", the children do reply
Now that's much better, Miss Jolly thinks, sitting with a sigh
Stop, Look and Listen, it's how to cross the road
No talking to strangers, is what they're all being told

So after all the minutes, and all the questions done
Wide-eyed children dismissed, off to have some fun
Pc Winn takes his hat, and places it under his arm
Secure now in the knowledge, he's helped keep them from harm.

Love & Relationships

A Gentle and Lonely One

At some point in our lives we all experience times and moments of great insecurity and emotional turmoil.

On reading this poem, look to take strength from the notion that you are not alone in such an experience. Many more have gone before you and many more will follow in your footsteps.

There will be moments of silence.

Make the most of those that offer support and reach out when all is out of your control.

A Gentle and Lonely One

Don't be sad, you must hold on
To a gentle and lonely one
He's scared and unsure too
Not knowing what to do

Don't be lonely, hang in there
Your not alone, so do not despair
He's lonely inside too
Hold on now, you'll both come through

The tunnel now, looks very long
So imagine your favourite love song
Sing it loud within your heart
Soon there will be a brand new start

Now you're there, hold on tight
Keep your love strong all through the night
So do not be sad, you must hold on
To that gentle and lonely one.

Happiness

Something that is becoming very natural at this present time in my writings is the ability to write a poem on a subject, usually at short notice and related to emotions or, a memorable event.

By using photographs, props, relationships and experiences, I have been known to produce some structure to the work within hours for stressed out friends and even would be clients in need of something different.

"Happiness" evolved from an original title of "3000 miles" which I penned for Amanda and Ray, on their beautiful Wedding Day, in October 2007. We travelled from England to the USA for the ceremony. Somehow "3000 miles" just did not suit the occasion and I think you will agree "Happiness" has that blissful ring to it.

With a little help from our friends in Michigan, we managed to find a local frame manufacturer, whom placed the written parchment within an exquisite standing glass frame, later finished off with a wrap of crossed lace for presentation.

Amanda and Ray are still very much in love and continuing to remain in Honeymoon Heaven.

Happiness

Three thousand miles to join you
On this your Special Day
To celebrate your marriage
We wouldn't have stayed away

An honour and a privilege
To share your sacred vows
Uniting all the families
In front of all the crowds

We take a quiet moment
To hear you say, "I do"
A wonderful beginning
Your lives to start anew

We wish you all the happiness
That life itself can bring
We wish you all the harmony
So you hearts can truly sing.

(For Amanda and Raymond)

Mom and Dad

I hold firm to my family values and often write about them within my poems. I feel strongly about commitment and love.

The poem 'Mom and Dad' was written for my parents on a milestone in life, their 50th (Golden) Wedding Anniversary.

Mom and Dad

Fifty years of marriage
From the day you said, "I do"
Fifty years of marriage
So much that you've both been through

Wonderful couples don't often exist
They're a glow in the dark, sun through the mist
Glad to share you, its warms our hearts
My Mom and Dad who won't be apart

Life has structured you'll be together
Sharing life's demands, betrothed forever
You've seen a lot, you'll see much more
Because that's the way your paths must fall

You tied the knot, and sealed your vows
A special day in front of the crowds
For richer for poorer, in sickness and in health
Your love for each other has been your wealth

That day was very sacred
For those who believe it true
A marriage for a lifetime
When you each betrothed "I do"

You've taught us many lessons
You've shown us love and care
Truly the very best parents
One could find anywhere.

Only Two

Incredibly, we can sometimes find strength from the most unexpected source.

Only Two

You held my hand when I cried
Touched my tears as they fell
Sat so still by my side
Those days I went through hell

So small and perfect your gestures
Each one an unselfish act
Your love came in huge measures
Our closeness my trial of tact

You bestowed your sympathy with measure
I opened my heart up to you
Those days felt like forever
Now gone like the morning dew

Your face would rest upon my arm
The still silence between us immense
The smile in your eyes would disarm
It was my only defence

I'd cry in the dark and you'd find me
No words for that came between
The gestures of love came silently
The relief was simply serene

I know I cannot thank you
Although it would be your due
My knight in shining armour
My little guy, you were only two.

The Elf and the Fairy

Indulge me for a moment - imagine yourself in a similar story to that of Peter Pan.

You may have love issues weighing on your mind.

In your dreams, you are there, trying to cope with those thoughts.

You try and figure out what to do, and what you would like to happen.

Amidst all of this, you find yourself listening in to a conversation between the Elf and the Fairy. They are talking about you.......

The Elf and the Fairy

Pinacled upon the edge, I feel
My soul spins around, as does a wheel

I'm so in love, this is true
I know not if my man loves me too

So distant as though, miles in between
My life, my love, my dream

Courage now is my valued friend
This I will keep until the end

My mind does talk amongst itself
Like the chattering Fairy and the Elf

Silently they whisper in my sleep
"Be brave now, and do not weep

Somewhere deep down, is your place
Although it shows not, upon his face

If you love him true, give him a chance
You'll soon see how, in that passing glance

Hold your love close and hold it dear
Soon your dreams, will be without fear"

That's what the Elf and Fairy tell me
Have faith and love, for eternity.

To Shed a Tear of Love

This poem is from the heart.

Upon reading it slowly a couple of times, its meaning begins to linger.

I see it as a blend of natural reactions interpreted with love and affection uppermost in my mind.

Putting it another way, when you have found true love, the feeling is enduring and it seeks to conquer all. Whether we all find eternal love with our partner is for each of us to discover.

I am very fortunate, I have been married for well over two decades.

I have a shining example in my parents' marriage, their love has endured for over fifty years. It is testimony, that there is someone out there for all of us to grow with, and with whom, to share our dreams.

To Shed a Tear of Love

To shed a tear of love
Comes from the aching heart
To shed a tear of sadness
Comes from spending time apart

They say love conquers all
Of this it is so true
Without it life would fall
Into the depths of mire and hue

Attachment to one another
Is a fixed and honoured thing
Detachment comes with sorrow
When ones heart can no longer sing

Beyond the realms of reality
Lie passions hard to find
Not just of sexuality
But of the deep and loving kind

Far away within ones dreams
Are desires so strong and true
They cannot command stage it would seem
For they are my secrets of you

Do not pass me by, or close your eyes
My deepest soul does exist
Within my heart where love lies
It's merely covered over by mist

There is a special time
When our souls will touch again
For the gladness in my mind
Will dance away the rain.

Memories

Down on the Beach

When we were children during the late Sixties and early Seventies, my parents would take the family on a day trip to the coastal town of Barmouth, in Wales.

A simple day out, but so enjoyable. This poem depicts a snippet of time, and some of my most favourite memories on the beach.

Down on the Beach

The 1960's, they were the best
Down on the beach, see grandad's string vest
Hankie on his head, trousers rolled high
Not a care in the world, it all flows by

Sand in our toes, sun on our backs
Ice cream in hand, newspapers on racks
Balls in baskets, buckets and spades on view
Fabulous times "Can we get one too?"

Building a castle, right there on the beach
Above in the sky, hear the seagulls screech
Plump old ladies, sit in their deck chairs
Laughing and chatting, they don't have a care

Holding our buckets, as we fished in the pools
Dip our hands in "Which crabs shall we choose?"
We all crouch down, to take a peek
"Quiet now" see the fish play hide and seek

Wrapped in a towel, sitting down on the ground
Sticky bun in our mouth and drinks beaker in hand
Egg sandwiches cut, into quarters to eat
Cup cakes and crisps, oh what a treat!

The day draws down, and the sun dips low
Pack up our things, it's now time to go
What a day, what fun, what a time we had
Remember the 60's, the best times, we're so glad.

I Remember

I have always maintained a close relationship with my parents.

Their support has been unwavering, and their wisdom something to behold.

I first wrote this poem within my Dad's 72nd Birthday card.

This poem is of memories, of my wonderful home and childhood during the late sixties, early seventies, and right on through experiences in adulthood.

I Remember

I remember hanging clothes out to dry
On the little washing line
I remember lots of playful times
With such a blissful sigh

I remember making snowmen
In our garden way back then
I remember long cold winters
And summers making a den

I remember very long journeys
In our Traveller, an all round view
I remember sleeping soundly
Those times were still brand new

I remember my Wendy house
One Christmas you built for me
I remember all the effort
Fond memories eternally

I remember being protected
From all the burly boys
I remember emotional times
You never made a noise

I remember when I married
On the day I said, "I do"
I remember our proud moment
When I began a time so new

I remember when you became a Grandad
Our son we showed to you
I remember how you loved him
With a Grandads' easy eye view

So it leaves us now to express
In each and every way
Much love and happiness
On this your Special Day

You are the very best
You've given so much joy
As your Dad was to you
You are our real McCoy.

Flying High

For anyone contemplating parasailing, otherwise known as parascending over the sea from a powerboat.

My husband finally persuaded the family to try it during a recent beach holiday. We paired up and took off from a boat in the resort bay.

It was a "WOW".

I hope my words may encourage you to try this exhilarating experience sometime.

Go on, be brave.

Flying High

Up into the air, we were sucked from the boat
Like sardines from a can, no longer afloat
It takes your breath, so you gulp in some air
Straight up to the sky, like a firework flare

Hold on tight, sit into the harness
Look out to sea, it's incredible calmness
The air whips up and around your face
Sea birds fly by, with amazing grace

Small boats in the distance, only a speck
So high up, we can't see the deck
We jump and bounce, as the wind passes over
If we keep on going, we could see Dover

Sweeping aloft, with the high white clouds
Look down to the beach, wave to the crowds
Reel us in, towards the deck
A scary manoeuvre, oh' what the heck

Land on the boat, which is bobbing around
Catch hold of the rail, we are safely down
Shall we come back? I think it's a must
Safely in hand, it's all down to trust

Speed back to land, now that we are through
In a shiny white boat, on the water we flew
No longer a speck or a dot, on the ocean
We land on the beach, with such a commotion

We alight from our boat and wade through the sea
Fish in the water swimming by me
Laughing and chatting, a race to the beach
Back to the hut, our destination is reached.

Plank Motor Kid

Totally inspired by my parents who had been bought up in the inner city of Birmingham, England, during the Second World War.

Their world was one of hardships, fear, ingenuity and moments of great adventure, in the bomb shelled houses looking for shrapnel and coal.

During recent years, the National Trust has started to preserve and restore some of the old Birmingham "Back to Back" dwellings of that period and beyond. There is a fine terrace of such dwellings and museum in Inge and Hurst Street, within Birmingham city centre.

The Trust has also been busy, archiving recorded narratives by people such as my parents for prosterity.

"Back in the Day" Plank Motors were cobbled together from packing cases and pram wheels. They served for childhood play in the backyards and were also vital for bringing home the spoils, from the markets and bomb-shelled streets.

My parents experiences, often recounted for their Grandchildren, have proved uplifting and inspiring, provoking me to put pen to paper.

By listening to their stories I have attempted to capture the atmosphere and dialect of those times.

Plank Motor Kid

Hear the plank motor, racing down our street
Over the cobbled road
"Look out our kid, watch your feet"

The charging noise, the excited air
"Who's gonna win?"
We don't have a care

Taken in turns, speed defies
We each get a go
"Lets race for the skies"

Won again, we got the best wheels
A quick glance back
They were hot at our heels

Down to the Market into the Bullring
Errands for Grandad
Now here's the thing

Get what we can, leftovers, and leaves
See Barrow Boys
On to the plank motor, whatever, they please

Our Grandad'll be chuffed
We got quite a lot
Chickens'll be fed, an' us stuffed

Our Mam sorts it out, we get the best
Into the pot
The chickens get the rest

Dig over their pen, me Grandads pleased
Bring up the coal
Down the cellar I'm squeezed

Excitin' to hear, the rumble in the sky
Sirens go off
Into the shelters we fly

Gas mask on back, boots to bare feet
"Christ" Mom thinks
"Hope its' not our street"

It's cloudy and dusty as we emerge
That stench in the air
Look at the bombed house on the verge!

Some do collapse, some hold their own
We go gathering shrapnel
Try to sneak it all home

So those were the days, the good and the bad
So many moments
We should've been sad!

Instead we were happy
We enjoyed every day
Rich with our treasures, our own special way

Now we are older, the memories we share
'Back to Back Houses'
Our own kids we take there

We revel in telling, how it was back then
Secure in our minds
We made soldiers of men

History won't stop, or fade away
Recording our times
Of each, every day

We reckon this world could do with a view
Of the days and the times
That we all went through

Stronger it made us, resilient in mind
A wonderful life
We won't ever leave behind.

Secret Waterfall

Memories are precious. There are so many things I recall.
I write them down and turn them into poetry.

This is one example of setting diary notes into verse.

Do you know this place? Have you been there too?

Secret Waterfall

I have an image in my minds eye
Of a day we spent in a time gone by
Me, with a handful of kids, and my mom and dad
What a day, what a time we had

Way up high in a secret place
I found it there, joy upon my face
From a cascading waterfall, so, so cool
I came upon a fresh swimming pool

Deep in the shade of a tree filled hill
No other place, would've fitted the bill
With squeals and hollers as they jumped in
Such a great time as they went for a swim

The pool wasn't deep, just fresh and clear
Swinging on a rope, keeping up the rear
The tiny island was set in the centre
A place to explore, a great adventure

They built a dam, and the water filled high
Then over the top, watch it 'whoosh' on by
We sat on the side, and ate ice cream
A scene from a book, a wonderful dream

Time to explore the surrounding land
Climbed up the hill, hand in hand
Get to the top and see the view
Stretching beyond the grass brand new

We went on a trek and yomped in deep
A line of little kids, looking out for sheep
Heading back now towards the meadow
See in the distance, the cars down below

Enter into the bracken and ferns
Smell the soil and tread the earth
It's cool and dark now out of the sun
Such a good time we are having fun

Holler at Grandad down by the stream
He looks up, can't see us, it would seem
We giggle and laugh and call again
Keep our heads down, such a good game

Down at the bottom, now to cool our feet
Dip our toes into the clear, cold, creek
The sun drops down behind the hill
Our day's done here, we've had our fill

I have this image in my minds eye
Of this day we spent in a time gone by
Of a handful of kids and my mom and dad
A fabulous day, a great time we had.

Unspoken Word

We all each and every one of us, at one time, or another, go through trauma, upset, and emotional times.

For me, I write about emotional times through poetry.

I wrote this for my Mom. She has been fighting Cancer for the fourth time in her life. There were things I needed her to know.

It felt special putting down my thoughts and feelings on paper.

In giving Mom a framed copy of the poem, it also helped me to show my love and admiration for her.

Unspoken Word

A world of inspiration, down the years you've always been
Any tears or sadness, have been kept away unseen
There are so many memories, of times I've had with you
Those memories are so clear, and will never leave my view

Your strength and your endurance, have always been the key
You've never failed or faltered, it's helped in moulding me
You listened when I needed you, I've cried upon your chest
When it's been necessary, you gave to me your best

My childhood was so wonderful, where summers were very long
Always spending time with us, your presence very strong
I smile, as I remember, making tents and pegging out the sheets
The hours we used to spend, you helped us make it neat

Our Christmas's were magical you put joy upon my face
Aromas from the kitchen, and flames in the fireplace
We may not have had a lot, but you know we never knew
To us it was so special, those times we had with you

On holiday, our Bedford van, you made a home from home
Down on the beach you joined us, we never played alone
A bucket in our hands, we'd trail along the beach
There amongst the rock pools, our destination reached

Those days are ours to treasure, and I need to say
You're still my inspiration, as I think of you each day
I marvel at your strength, and everything you know
Those days are not forgotten, they were times to learn and grow

That's exactly what I've done, to reach this point in life
Watched how to become a mother, and to be a wife
You shall always go before me, so I can aim to be
The very best mother, that is what you've been to me.

Seasons

Summer Unfolds

Summer Unfolds is reminding us all that we should let ourselves go, sometimes.

Give way and allow deep restrained emotions out, to explore their real and true meanings.... if only briefly.

Find someone to trust and talk to, the relief of sharing some of those feelings and emotions can lead to a peaceful mind.

Summer Unfolds

The rain has fallen
the grass is now green
meadows and street ways beckon
ready to be walked and seen

Birds twitter, waters run
pastures new, hilltops old
as so many before
the summer unfolds

Smell the trodden earth
dwell upon its scent
time to share feelings
that winter kept to tempt

Watch the world go by
sit beneath a tree
relax here with a sigh
only think of me

Warm sun upon your face
close your eyes a while
stay here for a moment
I love to see your smile.

Nature's Call

Inspired by nature and my home garden.

I love this poem. I feel compelled to write at this time of the year, in the Fall. I think it's because my birthday falls on the first day of autumn.

In describing the poem, I take the view it is a written photograph of what I see happening in my garden during the month of September.

Nature's Call

See the shed door, flap crossly in the wind
Watch the empty bird box, see it swing
The bright yellow bamboo sways to touch the pond
Its skims the top of the water, with each long frond

See the graceful grasses bow, to natures gentle breeze
Watch the bright Cyclamen, strong flowers above the leaves
Hear the wind chimes, make music to the sway
They jingle and jangle, bringing tunes to each day

See the strong Rosemary, majestic and tall
Watch it hold strong, as summer turns to Fall
Catch the fragrance, of the Mint and the Thyme
I'll take out my scissors, for they'll soon be mine

See the buds form, on tall Jasmine soon
Watch how in winter, yellow flowers festoon
The red Sedum and Cosmos, swaying around
Soon to be over, taken down to the ground

See how the clouds, race across grey skies
Watch how they form, hover, and then rush by
Strong summer sun fades, to glimpses of yellow
Replaced by leaves in the breeze, and hot days now mellow

See how nature calls, to make her world rest
Watch how she sheds leaves, colours at their best
The season has come for all to ease
Time for a change can be felt on the breeze.

Where Tulips Grow

I wrote this within hours of completing the poem - My Brother (Family Chapter) I produced this tribute for my husband at the time of the loss of his younger brother and, to remind him of happier times shared with both of his brothers.

My heart goes out to all who have lost someone they have loved, when taken from them forever, in such sudden circumstances.

By Paris..

Where Tulips Grow

As I gaze out onto the days of late September
I will have memories of a day, I do not wish to remember
My thoughts will go to where; I do not want to be
Where you had turmoil in your life, instead of harmony

So I will go to the patch of ground, where tulips nestle deep
Ready to burst forth in spring, it's where I'll go to weep
It's there that I will think of you and a time when we were lads
A time stored in my memory, that no one else can have

I shall take a moment to remember all those days of fun
To when we kicked a football, oops, we'd better run
Watch out for Grandad's roses and mind the veggie patch
God help us if we hit the house and break the window glass

We sat upon the sideboard and our legs they would not reach
Our hair was all combed down, and we were missing two front teeth
Two little boys in a photograph to keep for all of time
These are some of my memories which are now, just mine

I'll see hot days in Florida, when we were grown up men
Three thousand miles away, what a time we shared back then
A holiday of a lifetime, when we were brothers three
So many happy memories, one big family

I won't think of how you were taken, on that tragic day
It's just a place in time, where I do not wish to stay
I will fight to find a place, deep within my heart
A place of warmth and happiness, where brothers do not part

I need to let you know that in the quiet night
There is a place where we can meet, where it feels, just right
It's the ground where tulips grow and show themselves in spring
"Happy Birthday Sid" raising up their heads they'll sing

My brother you must rest, in this place you've gone to stay
It's where we will meet again, on some other day
I need to spend some time right here, because it feels so right
You are not so far away from me, for now it's just good night.

Step out into the Garden

'Step out into the garden' is a selection of words which I wrote down one afternoon whilst gazing out upon my own garden in Lichfield, in England. As I did so the realization of the season changing struck me and prompted this poem.

I have since felt that maybe one day, music could be put to these words to make it a song.

Go on, step out into the garden, and see what you can find.

Step out into the Garden

Step out into the garden, as autumn begins to fall
Step out into the garden, when nature comes to call

She's clever and resourceful, in each and every way
She never wastes a moment, of every changing day

Step out into the garden, gather up its scents
Step out into the garden, where summertime was spent

The long hot days are over, and changes are anew
Colour in the leaves, to be seen in every hue

Step out into the garden, and listen to the sounds
Step out into the garden, crispness on the ground

Fuchsias hanging there, geraniums holding tight
As wintertime does beckon, they hold on with all their might

Step out into the garden, feel fresh air upon your face
Step out into the garden, is a race to hibernate

Look up into the sky, and see the geese in flight
A long hard journey ahead, they flap with all their might

Step out into the garden, feel calm within your heart
Step out into the garden its natures, brand new start.

A to Z of Poems

A Gentle and Lonely One
A Million Times
Alexander
Autumn Breeze
Boulders on the Sea
Burning Bright
Call me Dad
Down on the Beach
Flying High
Forever
Gampa
Ghosts
Ha Ha
Happiness
Healthy Competition
Hope
I Recall
I Remember
I Wonder
Indian Spirit
Jigsaw, Jigsaw
La Gomera, My Island of Dreams
Land of the Indian Chief
Life's Folly
Mom and Dad
Moments
My Brother
My Little Brother Dreams Away
My Little Place of Paradise
My Love
Nancy's Mud
Nature's Call
Only Two
Our Robin
PC WINN

Acknowledgements

To . . . . .

Madeline Neumann, my "American Sister" a truly uplifting and strong lady.

Anni Bell, for being a huge emotional support in the turmoil of life.

Always in my thoughts.....
Saran and Jimmy McMaster, Margaret and Brian Goodman,
Yvonne and Barry Munn, Jean Johnston, Helen Walker and family,
Margaret Heap, Dave and Marylin Smith, Ruth Parnell and family,
Ann and Bob Ling, Freda and Eric Taylor.
Bob and Suzy Young, Carol Pickles, Keith Hughes, David MeGrath,
Rich and Sandy Jones.

George Kovtun Principal at St. Peters School for making us so welcome.

Vicki and Mick Conway for providing a Canary Island retreat.

Tom McNulty for all your tutoring, computers, support and humour
(Microman Computer Support at tom@micromancs.com)

Liam Brandom at AuthorHouse, for providing a pleasant and professional introduction to this new adventure.

Glossary

Barrow Boy: a man or boy who sells fruit, vegetables etc from a barrow.

Cancer: a very serious disease.
Macmillan Cancer Research – www.macmillan.org.uk

Cellar: basement room.

Coastguard: a force employed to guard the coast.

Gas Mask: a piece of equipment worn over the face to protect from poisonous gases.

Holler: to shout loudly.

McCoy: the real McCoy: something that is real and is not a copy, especially something valuable.

Native American Indian: Someone who belongs to one of the races that lived in North America before Europeans arrived. For more information visit Smithsonian Institute Washington DC. USA.

Robin: rob'in. erithacus rubecula. European bird. Often referred to as "robin redbreast".

Shrapnel: pieces of metal from a bomb or bullet for example, that are scattered when it explodes.

Siren(s): a piece of equipment that makes very loud warning sounds.

Wendy house: a children's playhouse

Yoga: a system of exercises that help control mind and body in order to relax.

References

Barmouth, Wales: Tourist Board: www.barmouth-wales.co.uk

Bedford (CF) van: manufactured by Vauxhall Motors. A favourite vehicle for camper conversions, usually with aftermarket roof extensions.

Birmingham, West Midlands: The heart of Middle England, often referred to as the country's second city.

Bullring: original markets in Birmingham city centre.

Charter Township of Clinton Police Department
37985 Groesbeck Highway, Clinton TWP, Michigan, 48036, USA.
911 Services, Law Enforcement, Public Safety.
Honor Guard c/o Police Lt. Raymund Macksoud.
www.clintontownship-mi.gov/police

Cromwell: 1599-1658. Oliver Cromwell became Lord Protector in 1653 of England, Scotland and Ireland.

Dover: South-East England port, also famous for its White Cliffs (of Dover).

Dr Samuel Johnson Society, (Birthplace) Market Street, Lichfield
www.samueljohnsonbirthplace.org.uk

Erasmus Darwin. Darwin House Museum, Beacon Street, Lichfield.
www.erasmusdarwin.org

Flowers and plants . . . .

Bamboo: pronounced bam'bu. Tall tropical plant with hollow stems that grows in many climates and also has many practical uses.

Cosmos: pronounced cosmos. Herbaceous perennial with deep burgundy flowers, smelling of chocolate.

Cyclamen: pronounced Sic'lamen. Perennial plant.

Fuchsia: pronounced fu'shi-a. Annual, Perennial flowering plants and shrubs.

Geranium: pronounced je-ra'ni-um. Annual, flowering bedding plant.

Jasmine: jasmine nudiflorum. pronounced jas'min. Deciduous plant, climbing shrub, with fragrant yellow flowers.

Mint: pronounced mint. Herbaceous aromatic plant. Has culinary uses.

Rosemary: pronounced roz'ma-ri. Evergreen shrub yielding a fragrant essential oil. Has culinary uses.

Sedum: pronounced sedum. Herbaceous perennial plant.

Thyme: pronounced time. Small aromatic shrub. Has culinary uses.

Tulips: pronounced tu'lip. Perennial bulbs, of the lily family, in rich variety of colours.

La Gomera and Tenerife, Canary Islands, Spain: www.turismodecanarias.com

Lichfield: Cathedral City in South Staffordshire, England. Lichfield Cathedral, The Close, Lichfield, Staffordshire. www.lichfield-cathedral.org

National Trust. Back to Back Houses Museum. 50-54 Inge Street junction 55-63 Hurst Street, Birmingham, West Midlands. B5 4TE. www.nationaltrust.org.uk

Keith Neumann, Patrolman, Essex County Police, New Jersey. USA. Officer Down Memorial Page www.odmp.org

Saint Chad (St.Chad): c634 – 672. 7th Century Anglo Saxon Churchman.

St.Peter's Evangelical Lutheran School and Church, Richmond, Michigan.

Traveller: (Austin Morris Minor Traveller, Series II) an estate version of the famous Morris Minor saloon car made by car manufacturer Austin Morris Motors between 1952 and 1971.

Washington Police Week: National Law Enforcement Officers Memorial Fund (N.L.E.O.M.F) USA. Chairman Mr Craig Floyd www.nleomf.com

WWI First World War: 1914 - 1918.
WWII Second World War: 1939 - 1945.

Thank you for reading my first book

Look out for my next title

" My Place"

Visit my Website for details

http://www.suzannestone.co.uk/

www.authorhouse.com

www.authorhouse.co.uk

Printed in the United Kingdom by
Lightning Source UK Ltd., Milton Keynes
141601UK00002BA/19/P